52 WEEKS
OF FAMILY
GERMAN

Eileen Mc Aree

CONTENTS

Introduction

Learning a foreign language is a wonderful goal, and it can also be a fun and rewarding experience. What stops many people from attempting to learn a foreign language is their own fear of speaking, of looking foolish in front of another person. They may be comfortable studying vocabulary lists or grammar rules, but without actually speaking a language, no one can really progress. *52 Weeks of Family German* is designed to get you speaking German from the very first day!

Not only will you build on your own success as you learn to communicate in German, you will take your children along on this exciting journey. Children are naturally curious and full of enthusiasm. They haven't yet faced a conjugated verb or a double negative. They have no idea that learning to speak a foreign language is supposed to be difficult. What better study partners could you ask for? For most of us, our inhibitions about pronouncing foreign words disappear when we practice with our children. Using the simple lessons provided in this book, you and your children will be speaking to each other (and hopefully other people) in German quickly and easily.

52 Weeks of Family German is designed to be a relaxed, self-teaching guide. Each week you focus on a simple conversational concept that you and your children can practice together. The conversations were chosen based on their relevance to real, everyday family life. The lessons are short and simple and will get you and your family practicing German in the many of the moments modern families share together: mealtimes, morning "rush hour", carpools, bedtime. This is an oral introduction to the German language, so there are no spelling rules to memorize or flashcards to flip. Grammar is touched on throughout the curriculum but the main goal is to get you and your family speaking this beautiful language.

Features of the Book

Before you begin, take a look through the book. There are several features that will make the learning process easier for both you and your children.

- **Words and Phrases to Get You Started**
  This is a small compilation of some words and phrases you should know from the beginning to encourage and instruct your children.

- **52 Week Curriculum**

  This is the heart of it all, and when you see how simple each week's lesson is, you may be surprised. Certain weeks focus on only one phrase! The fact is that fifty-two small, achievable lessons add up to quite a store of conversational skills, and conversation is the ultimate goal of this book. It was written to provide a family with a respectable oral vocabulary in about a year. Exactly how fast your family progresses is entirely up to you. If you and your kids are in a groove and you want to move ahead, by all means follow the momentum. On the other hand, if you are dealing with an ear infection, an impending dance recital and a huge deadline at work, stretch one week's lesson into three weeks. The pace is yours to decide. You and your family will be successful if you simply *keep talking*.

- **Suggested Activities**

  As every busy parent knows, it is not always easy to find time to go to the supermarket, let alone learn *and teach* a brand new language. This section is full of realistic, fun and engaging ways to practice your German skills in the context of your everyday life.

- **Resources**

  Listed here are many wonderful materials available to make learning a foreign language fun and engaging. The internet makes it possible to access many educational games for free. For those with "smart" phones, there are apps that can reinforce language learning while you wait outside school, in a fast food pick up line, or entertain a younger sibling at baseball practice. Also listed here are some books and CD's that can further pique your child's interest in the German language.

How to Use This Book

1. **52 Weeks of Family German** follows an auditory and oral learning model. Listening to the sounds of a new language and communicating successfully in that language opens the mind to a new structure of thinking. Vocabulary drills and grammar rules shut down the learning process at this early stage. This is not to imply vocabulary and grammar are not crucial to the mastery of any language. It is simply that to get the process started, *the natural way is to start talking*.

2. **Talk, Talk, Talk!** Use your new vocabulary every day, even it is only for a one minute conversation. You will be surprised and pleased to see how a minimal time commitment, *every day*, leads to the attainment of a great deal of vocabulary.

3. **Watch your pronunciation**. Try to correct any major pronunciation errors as soon as they occur. The pronunciation guides should help you with this. The faster you correct yourself, the faster you will learn.

4. **Touch on each week's** *cultural note*. Every week's lesson includes a fact about about German culture. Introducing children to German culture increases their curiosity about the language. It makes the process more interesting and fun for you as well!

5. **Take time to review**. Review weeks are built into the curriculum. Take your time! If you feel you and your family haven't mastered one week's concept, continue your review till you are ready to move on.

6. **Remember, it's a journey, not a race**. Many language courses advertise mastery of a language in record time. Babies don't learn to talk overnight, and people don't speak new languages overnight either. Your German speaking skills will continue to improve as long as you keep speaking and learning. Enjoy!

Suggested Activities

1. **Short and sweet conversations**. Each week's lesson is bite size German concept that you can review during a five minute conversation. Resist the impulse to drill, if your child forgot a word, just provide it for them. The repetition of language will help their vocabulary grow. Great places for bite-sized conversations are:

   - In the car…all parents spend plenty of time in the car! Use this time to squeeze in some language learning.
   - At mealtimes…many of the lessons in this book are perfect to review before breakfast, lunch or dinner…or snack at the pool…or a snack in the mall…..
   - Bedtimes…start with "*Ich liebe dich* (I love you.)" and move on from there!
   - "Downtime"…Waiting in the pediatrician's examination room, waiting for your food to be delivered at Chili's, anytime or place you need to kill five minutes, use it to review German!

2. **Put on the radio.** By putting on German language CD or podcast in the car or kitchen while you make dinner, you acclimate your ear, and your children's if they are listening, to the rhythm and cadence of German speech. You are hearing native or fluent speakers provide an accent model.

3. **Find a German language children's TV show.** Children's television shows are not terribly complicated in terms of character and plot, and you can derive meaning just by watching. Many familiar children's television shows are available online in German.

4. **Read a bilingual storybook.** In the Resources section of this book, you will find websites that can help you locate children's picture books in both English and German. The plots are simple so you can get a lot of meaning from the picture clues. Also, reading aloud to your children helps you work on your accent.

5. **Say hello!** One of the hardest parts of learning a new language is overcoming our own embarrassment and communicating with native speakers. If you can get over this hurdle you will have conquered a challenge that turns many people away from learning a second language. In certain areas of the world, it may be easy to meet German speaking people. In others, it is difficult to find anyone who speaks German at all. Utilize the internet to locate groups of fellow German language learners.

6. **Make friends.** One of the benefits of learning about a new culture and language is meeting new friends. Whether you meet a local mother at the playground who hails from Berlin or you need to utilize the internet to find language partners, you will surely enrich your life with the new and interesting people you will meet.

7. **Start a playgroup.** If you are a take charge kind of person, start your own playgroup! No matter where in the world you live, you can guarantee there are other parents interested in teaching their children a second language. Internet sites like Meetup.com are great tools for creating playgroups.

8. **Play.** Have fun with German. The Resources section lists lots of fun games, books and CD's to support your learning. In addition, try playing the following vocabulary review games with your kids:

- *Wo ist (voh eest)?* Ask your children where different items in the room are. They recognize the vocabulary word and point to the item.

- *Heiss oder Kalt (hiss oh-dehr kahlt)?* This is your basic game of hot or cold except instead of hiding an object in the room, you *think* of an item in the room. You then direct your children toward it with cues of *heiss oder kalt.* The child who figures out which item you were thinking of (lamp, television, etc.) must call out the name of the item in German.

- *Mama (Papa) hat gesagt, "Fass an Dein/Deine..." (mah-mah (pah-pah) haht geh-sahgt, « fahss ahn din/dine... »)* Here is a version of Simon says. Mommy (or Daddy) says to touch different body parts, items in the room, items of clothing etc. Children must understand the vocabulary they are hearing in order to act accordingly. They are out if they touch something and Mama didn't say!

- *Zwanzig Fragen (zvahn-zig frah-jhehn) .* Children are given the opportunity to ask twenty questions to figure out the item you are thinking of. They can ask questions about it in English (or German as their knowledge increases) but they have to guess what it is in German.

- *Ich sehe was, was Du nicht siehst. Und das ist...(eech zeh-eh vahs, vahs dooh neecht zeeh-st. oohnd dahs eest...)* This literally reads: I see something you don't see. And that is... Play this game the same way you would play *I Spy*. As your vocabulary increases you can use more and more German describing words to help your children puzzle out what you see.

- *Puppets.* Puppets are an invaluable tool for teaching language. Buy or make a hand puppet, name your puppet (Try German names to go with your theme!), and make the puppet your German teacher's helper. Anytime you want to review dialog, take out your puppet and talk away. Older children can help put on the puppet show for younger children.

- *Beanbag Toss*. This is simply another way to review vocabulary. Get a beanbag (or soft, small ball, or stuffed animal, anything that won't go through a window or cause a concussion). The first person says a word or phrase in German and tosses the beanbag to the next person who then has to give the translation. If they don't get the correct answer, they are out. If they do get the correct answer, they come up with another German phrase and toss the beanbag to the next person. You can reverse this activity and say the words or phrases in English and have the children provide the German translation. That is always a little harder!

Words and Phrases to Get You Started

As an individual, you are embarking on a journey to learn German. As a parent, you are additionally taking on the role of teacher. With this knowledge in mind, prepare yourself from day one with some basic vocabulary that will guide and encourage your children. It also adds to the language they will pick up through exposure!

Sehr gut! (zehr gooht):	Very good!
Phantastisch! (fahn-tahs-teesh):	Fantastic!
Traumhaft! (trowm-hahft):	Wonderful!
Sag das nochmal! (sahg dahs nohch-mahl):	Tell me again.
Kannst Du das bitte wiederholen?	Repeat, please.
(kahnst dooh dahs bee-teh vee-dehr-hoh-lehn)	
Versuch(t) es nochmal! (talking to 1(multiple) person(people) *fehr-soohch(t) ehs nohch-mahl).:*	Try again.
Pass(t) auf!(pahss owf):	Pay attention!
Beruhige Dich!(beh-roohi-geh deech):	Calm down.
Warte(t)! (wahr-teh(t)):	Wait.
Komm(t) her! (kohm(t) hehr):	Come here.
Gute Arbeit! (gooh-the ahr-bit):	Good job!
Hör(t) (mir) zu! (hur(t) meer tsooh):	Listen to me.
In einer Sekunde!(een i-nehr zeh-koohn-deh):	In a second….

And don't forget……*Ich liebe Dich!* …..I love you!

(eech lee-beh deech)

52 Week Curriculum

Here is an overview of how the weeks of your year of learning German are divided. Topics were chosen for ease of learning and application to real life. Suggested reviews are included in each week's lesson. Don't feel compelled to go in order! If you want to learn how to say, "I'm hungry!" in German, by all means skip straight to Unit 5. Remember, go in an order that is interesting to you and at a speed you and your family are comfortable with. This book was written to make German learning easy and fun!

Unit 1: Weeks 1-8
Theme: Making Friends
Cultural Spotlight: Introducing German

Unit 2: Weeks 9-16
Theme: All About Me
Cultural Spotlight: A Child's Life in German

Unit 3: Weeks 17-24
Theme: Welcome to My Home
Cultural Spotlight: German Art and Music

Unit 4: Weeks 25-32
Theme: Useful Information
Cultural Spotlight: German Food

Unit 5: Weeks 33-40
Theme: Mealtimes
Cultural Spotlight: Famous German People

Unit 6: 41-48
Theme: Getting Ready
Cultural Spotlight: German Culture Around the World

Unit 7: Weeks 49-52
Theme: A Few Odds and Ends
Cultural Spotlight: Fun German Facts!

Unit 1: Making Friends

Week 1: Manners

Vocabulary:

ja/nein   (yes/no)
yah/nine

bitte   (please)
bett-eh

danke   (thanks)
dahn-keh

vielen Dank   (thank you very much)
feel-en dahnk

gern geschehen (you're welcome)
gehrn geh-sheh-ehn

Pronunciation note: Many letter sounds in German differ from the letter sounds in English. Throughout this book you will see explanations of different pronunciations. Here are some examples:

In German usually every letter is spoken, none are silent. An "h" or an "e" behind another vowel indicates the vowel needs to be spoken slightly longer- b**ee** rather than b**eh.**

An "a" in a word is said like the British "a" in bath.

The "e" is said like the first "e" in fence, and an "e" at the end of the word is always spoken, never silent.

The combination of "ei" is a special sound close to the "i" in nine.

The sounds for "i" is close to the "i" in bitter and the sound for "ie" is the same as the "ee" sound in bee.

The "g" sound is spoken like in garden or like a soft "k".

If you are reading German, you will see the letter ß, the *esszet*. This is pronounced like a double ss, and for simplicity's sake, in this book a ss is used.

Finally, the sound for "j" is like in "yes" or "yard".

Cultural Note: Germany is located in the center of the European continent. It borders nine other countries…more than any other European country! Germany has a stunning landscape that includes mountains, forests and coastlines.

Idea! Use your new manners words at mealtimes. Pair the English word of whatever you want with the German manners word. Encourage your children to do the same. Don't worry about mixing up the languages, that's how communication is born.

Week 2: Greetings

Review: Week 1: Manners

Vocabulary:

Guten Tag   (hello)
Gooh-tehn-tahg

Auf Wiedersehen   (goodbye)
Owf vee-dehr-zehn

Guten Morgen   (Good morning)
Gooh-tehn mohr-gehn

Guten Abend   (Good evening)
Gooh-tehn ah-behnd

Pronunciation note:. The combination of "au" represents a sound like the "ou" in mouse. The "w" is spoken like in vine.

Cultural Note: The capital of Germany is Berlin. The country of Germany is made up of sixteen *landers*, or states.

Idea! Teaching your kids to not only say "please" and "thank you", but "hello" and "goodbye" to adults they encounter is a great lesson in manners. Saying it in German is bonus!

Week 3: Introductions

Review: Week 2: Greetings

Vocabulary:

Wie geht es Ihnen/Dir?	(How are you)
Vee geht ehs Ee-nehn/Deer	
Es geht mir gut.	(good)
Ehs geht meer gooht	
Und Ihnen/Dir?	(and you?)
Oohd Ee-nehn/Deer	

Grammar note: In Germany, a polite form of *you* is used to address people , *Ihnen* . It is distinct from a form for people who know each other or when addressing children, *Dir.*

Cultural Note: The city of Berlin is thought to be over 700 years old! In the past century, it was divided into East Berlin and West Berlin by the Berlin Wall. Once the wall came down, unified Berlin began to thrive as a center of arts and commerce.

Idea! Have fun role playing out a simple conversation with your children.

Guten Tag. Wie geht es Dir?

Es geht mir gut, danke. Und Dir?

Gut, danke.

Week 4: What's Your Name?

Review: Week 2: Greetings

Vocabulary:

> Wie heissen Sie? (What is your name ?)
> *Vee hi-ssehn see*

> Ich heisse_____. (My name is_____.)
> *Ich hi-sseh_____.*

Grammar note: There is a formal you, *sie,* and an informal you, *du,* in German. Since you don't know a stranger, here we are using the formal you, *sie.* Literally, we are asking, "What are you called?"

Cultural note: The mountains of northern Germany are heavily forested. Many German folktales speak of spooky magical creatures living in these dark woods.

Idea! Velvet rope your kitchen! Before dinner or other mealtime where you are not too rushed, hang a streamer across the kitchen door and before children can enter they must answer the question, *"Wie heissen Sie?"* You can pretend you don't know each other!

Week 5: How Old Are You?

Review: Week 4: What is Your Name?

Vocabulary:

> Wie alt bist Du?   (How old are you?)
> *Vee ahlt beest dooh*
>
> Ich bin _____ jahre alt.   (I am _____ years old.)
> *Ich been ___ yah-reh alt.*

Pronunciation note: The combination of "ch" is typically spoken somewhat like a soft "k" sound. Try using "Ick" for *Ich.* It is a uniquely German sound, but can also be spoken like "sh" and would then resemble someone with a heavy southern German dialect.

Cultural Note: Have you ever heard of the "Blue Danube"? The Danube is a river that runs from Germany's Black Forest on through Europe to the Black Sea in Romania.

Idea! Teach your child the German number for their age. Then interview each other as if you just met using the vocabulary from the previous lessons. Siblings can interview each other!

Week 6: More Greetings

Review: Week 3, Introductions

Vocabulary:

Wie geht's?	(How's it going?)
Vee gehts	
Und Du?	(and you?)
Oohnd dooh	
Bis bald/später!	(See you soon/later!)
Bees bahld/spah-tehr	

Grammar note: In German, there is a formal and informal way to address others. In Week 2, you learned the formal way to greet neighbors, coworkers or the way children would address adults. *"Wie geht's?"* is the more relaxed way of greeting one another. You could say this to friends or people you feel comfortable with. *Du* is the informal way of saying you.

Cultural note: The Bavarian Alps are Germany's portion of the Alpine Mountain range. These beautiful mountains are located in southern Germany and are one of the most spectacular areas of the country.

Idea! Incorporate these new phrases into your everyday life. *"Wie geht's?"* can be used every day while checking to see how the kid's homework is coming along. *"Bis später!"* is a great way to say goodbye before leaving for work in the morning.

Week 7: Nice to Meet You!

Review: Week 4: What's Your Name?

Vocabulary:

> Sehr erfreut!   (It's nice to meet you!)
> *zehr ehr-froid.*

Grammar note: The combination of "eu" always makes a sound like "oi" in void or voice.

Cultural note: The second largest city in Germany is Hamburg. Hamburg is home to more bridges than any other city in Germany.

Idea! Let your family pretend they have never met. They can make up new names and ages. Let them experiment with the conversational phrases they learned in the last few weeks. Make sure they end their role play conversations with, *"Sehr erfreut!"*.

Week 8: Review

- **Review:** all basic conversational vocabulary.

    o Use dolls or puppets to role play introductions.

- It can be challenging in some parts of the world to find people with whom to speak German. Try posting a notice at your local library for German study buddies (children or adults!). You will see that there are German students located in every corner of the globe!

- Learn more about Germany!

    o Go to a German restaurant.
    o Read about the printing press – one of the greatest modern inventions was created in Germany.
    o Go to a department store and smell some cologne. The first bottled cologne was sold in Germany hundreds of years ago in the town of Cologne.
    o Utilize the internet to "tour" some of the famous sights of Germany.
    o Color in a German flag.
    o Play soccer! There are many world class soccer (or *foossball)* players in Germany.

Unit 2: All About Me

Week 9: Who Am I?

Review: Basic conversation from Week 1-8.
Vocabulary:

Wer sind Sie/bist Du?	(Who are you?)
Vehr zeend zee/beest dooh	
Ich bin ein Mädchen.	(I am a girl.)
eech been in mad-chehn	
Ich bin eine Frau.	(I am a girl.)
eech been in-e frow	
Ich bin ein Junge.	(I am a boy.)
eech been in yoohn-geh	
Ich bin _____.	(I am *insert name.)*
eech been_____.	

Grammar note: When speaking German, words change depending on gender. There are two genders (he, she) and a third (it). To say "a" we use the word *ein* when we are talking about a girl (the article for mädchen is "it"), and *eine* when talking about a woman. We use the article *ein* when we are talking about a boy.

Cultural note: Students in Germany typically only go to school till twelve or one o'clock. They get plenty of homework though!

Idea! Take turns answering the question, *"Wer bist Du?"*. Encourage your children to also use previously learned vocabulary (ex: it would also be appropriate to respond, Ich heisse_____). If your children would like to expand on the lesson, look up the translation of something he or she loves to do.

Examples: *Ich bin eine Tänzerin :* I am a dancer.

                      Ich bin ein Künstler: I am an artist.

Remember to watch your use of gender!

Week 10: Feelings

Review: Week 3: Introductions
Vocabulary:

> Ich fühle mich gut.   (I am happy.)
> *eech fue-leh meech gooht.*
>
> Ich bin traurig.   (I am sad.)
> *eech been trow-reeg*

Grammar note: The *umlaute,* or *ä, ö,* and *ü* have special sounds that differ from the sounds of their corresponding vowels. These letter sounds do not really exist in the English language.

Cultural note: When children in Germany first begin school, they are given a *schultüte*, or "school cone". It is a paper or plastic cone filled with candy, small toys and school supplies.

Idea! Have your children make exaggerated faces while they say in German whether they are happy or sad.

Week 11: What Do I Look Like?

Review: Week 9: Who Am I?

Vocabulary:

Ich bin *eech been*	(I am)
gross *grohss*	(tall)
klein *klin*	(short)
hübsch *huebsh*	(pretty)
gutaussehend *gooht-ows-zeh-ehnd*	(handsome)

Grammar note: In German there is no change for the "I am" sentences, but there are changes if you are talking about a tall woman vs. a tall man or a tall "it".

Cultural note: German children love fun just as much as you. Germany is full of fun places for kids to visit with their families, like amusement parks with roller coasters, water parks, museums and zoos.

Idea! Use your cell phone to call your house phone. Let your kids chat to one another, greeting each other and describing themselves in German.

Week 12: What Do I Look Like?

Review: Week 11: What Do I Look Like?

Vocabulary:

> Ich habe blonde Haare   (I have blond hair.)
> *eech hah-beh blohn-deh hah-reh*
>
> Ich habe braune Haare   (I have brown hair)
> *eech hah-beh brow-neh hah-reh*
>
> Ich habe rote Haare   (I have red hair.)
> *eech hah-beh roh-teh hah-reh*
>
> Ich habe schwarze Haare.   (I have black hair.)
> *eech hah-beh shvahr-tseh hah-reh*

Grammar note: Nouns and people usually start with a capital letter.

Cultural note: In early spring, many German families participate in *Karneval,* also known as *Fastnach* or *Fasching*. The idea of Karneval dates back hundreds of years. Farmers would dress up in scary masks to scare away winter spirits and welcome spring. Parades and festivals are held to this day, and people still dress up and celebrate.

Idea! Have your children draw a self portrait. They can then use their new vocabulary to describe what they have drawn.

Week 13: What I Like to Do

Review: Weeks 11-12: What Do I Look Like?

Vocabulary:

Was machst Du gern?   (What do you like to do ?)
Vahs mahchst dooh gehrn

Ich lese gern.   (I like to read.)
Eech leh-zeh gehrn

Ich schwimme gern.   (I like to swim.)
Eech shvim-eh gehrn

Grammar note: Verbs are words that tell about things we can do. In German sentences the verb usually follows the subject directly. Translations between languages are not exact. A loose translation of this phrase would be "I read gladly (or with pleasure)". The meaning is, "I like to read."!

Cultural note: Most schools in Germany do not have sports teams. Instead, to participate in sports, German children join sports clubs.

Idea! Have each child pick their own activity they like to do (not listed above). Help them look up the German verb online or in a French dictionary and make their own sentence. Suggestions: *tanzen (to dance), singen (to sing), Fussball spielen (to play soccer), (mit dem) Computer spielen (to play on the computer).*

Week 14: My Face

Review: Weeks 11 and 12: What Do I Look Like?:

Vocabulary:

Fass Dein(e).......an. (Touch your...)

(die) Nase (nose)
dee nah-zeh ....ahn

(das) Gesicht (face)
dahs geh-zeecht

(der) Mund (mouth)
dehr moohnd

(die) Augen (eyes)
dee ow-gehn

(die) Ohren (ears)
dee oh-rehn

Pronunciation note: In German, when we use the word "your", we have to decide whether to be familiar or formal. Here we are using the familiar "your". However, you still have to match your pronoun "your" to the object's gender and number. For this reason, you would say,

Fass Deine Nase an (female, singular),

Fass Deinen Mund an (male, singular),

and *Fass Deine Augen an* (plural).

Don't worry if you mix up your pronouns at this early stage of learning, but try and practice "matching" the right form of "your" with different parts of the face.

Cultural note: Many of your favorite children's books came from Germany. *Grimm's Fairy Tales*, *Inkheart* and *The Neverending*

Story were all written by German authors.

Idea! Play a version of "Simon Says" called *"Mama hat gesagt"*. This is a game you can play anywhere to review vocabulary. *"Mama hat gesagt: Fass Deine Nase an!"* Remember, if Mama didn't say…you are out!

Week 15: My Body

Review: Week 14: My Face

Vocabulary:

(der) Kopf *dehr kohpf*	(head)
(der) Arm *dehr ahrm*	(arm)
(der) Fuss *dehr foohss*	(foot)
(das) Bein *dahs bin*	(leg)
(die) Hand *dee hahnd*	(hand)

Grammar note: To use the word "the" correctly in German, you must know if the object is considered masculine, feminine or neutral.

Der is "the" for masculine objects: the foot is *der Fuss*.

Die is "the" for feminine objects: the hand is *die Hand*.

Das is "the" for neutral objects: the leg is *das Bein*.

Cultural note: Germans often greet each other with a handshake. Even children shake hands upon meeting someone.

Idea! Expand on your "*Mama hat gesagt*" game to include parts of the body.

Week 16: Review

- Review all vocabulary from the past eight weeks.

    o Role play conversations
    o Draw self portraits and describe
    o Point out other people and pretend to be them. How would they describe themselves?

- Learn more about German family life.

    o Introduce your children to the world of Grimm's Fairy Tales. These traditional tales are scarier than their Disney counterparts so be prepared!
    o Play a game of *Topfschlagen*. In this traditional German party game, a small treat is placed in a pot and the pot is placed somewhere on the floor of the room. The first player is blindfolded and must search for the pot by hitting the floor with a cooking spoon. The other children shout out directions while he searches. Once the child finds the pot he gets to keep the treat!
    o German parties often have a punch bowl. Make your own fruit punch with your kids.
    o Is your child interested in knights, castles and princesses? Take an internet tour of Germany's Castle Road to see many of the beautiful and interesting castles that dot Germany's landscape.
    o German children love and utilize technology as much as any other country. Set up an email pen pal for your child (supervised, of course!).

Unit 3: Welcome to My Home

Week 17: Welcome to My Home

Review: Weeks 9-16

Vocabulary:

> Wilkommen (in meinem Heim)! (Welcome to my home!)
> *Weel-koh-mehn (een mi-nehm hows)*

Pronunciation note: Remember that every letter is spoken and always pronounced in the same way.

Cultural note: Have you ever heard of the Waltz? If you have ever seen a movie where there is ballroom dancing, then you have probably seen this classic dance. It is believed to have originated in southern Germany.

Idea! Take the plunge! Invite someone over, drum up your courage and welcome them in German. If you feel corny, don't worry. The more you use your German, the more natural it feels.

Week 18: Where Is It?

Review: Week 17: Welcome to my home!

Vocabulary:

Wo ist.....?   (Where is......?)
Voh eest

das Badezimmer (bathroom)
dahs bah-deh-tsee-mehr

die Küche   (kitchen)
dee kue-cheh

der Keller   (basement)
dehr keh-lehr

Grammar note: Remember, German nouns are either masculine, feminine, or neutral. Is *das Zimmer* masculine, feminine, or neutral? How about *die Küche*?

Cultural note: Bavarian folk music is popular in many parts of the world. Typically, the songs are played by a band and tell stories of everyday German life.

Idea! Practice using *"Wo ist...?"* with words you already know. This is a quick and easy way to practice.

"Wo ist (insert your child's name)?"

"Wo ist Deine Nase?"

Week 19: Where Is _____?

Review: Week 18: Where Is... ?

Vocabulary:

> der Tisch   (table)
> *dehr teesh*
>
> der Stuhl   (chair)
> *dehr stoohl*
>
> die Tür   (door)
> *dee tuer*
>
> das Fenster   (window)
> *dahs fehns-tehr*

Pronunciation note: Remember all letters in a German word are spoken. However, an "h" following a vowel indicates that the vowel should be pronounced a little longer..b*ee*t vs b*e*t.

Cultural note: The music of Bach is some of the most enduring music of our world. Even if you think you know nothing about classical music, you would probably recognize many of his pieces, like *Tocata and Fugue in A Minor.*

Idea! Have a treasure hunt! Hide some prizes (something small, an m&m, or sticker) in spots around your house. Say; "*Wo ist der Tisch?*" for example, and let your child claim the prize when they find the right object.

Week 20: Meet My Family (A)

Review: Week 19: Where is it?

Vocabulary:

> Das ist mein Vater.　　　(This is my father.)
> *Dahs eest min fah-tehr*

> Das ist meine Mutter.　　(This is my mother.)
> *Dahs eest mi-neh mooh-tehr*

Grammar note:. In German "it is", "this is", or "that is" can be expressed as *es ist, dies ist*, or *das ist*.

Cultural note: Woodcarving is an art form is Germany dating back hundreds of years. German wood carvers have created masterpieces out of the fronts of houses, altars, religious items, clocks and much more.

Idea! At dinner let your kids have fun presenting their mom or dad.

Week 21: Meet My Family (B)

Review: Week 20: Meet My Family (A)

Vocabulary:

Wer ist das?	(Who is this?)
vehr eest dahs	
Das ist mein Bruder.	(This is my brother.)
dahs eest min brooh-dehr	
Das ist meine Schwester.	(This is my sister.)
dahs eest mi-neh shvehs-tehr	

Pronunciation note: In German, all letters at the end of words are spoken. The emphasis is usually on the syllable before the last: `brou-der, wasch-ma-`schi-ne (washer; washing machine); but the last syllable is never silent.

Cultural note: Parsifal is a famous opera created by German composer Richard Wagner. It tells the story of a knight's quest in the time of King Arthur.

Idea! Car practice: Have your children take turns "introducing" everyone in the car .

Week 22: Meet My Family (C)

Review: Weeks 20 and 21:Meet My Family (A and B)

Vocabulary:

die Oma (Grossmutter)		(grandmother)
dee oh-mah		
der Opa (Grossvater)		(grandfather)
dehr oh-pah		
die Tante		(aunt)
dee than-teh		
der Onkel		(uncle)
dehr ohn-kehl		
der/die Cousin(e)		(cousin)
dehr cooh-zehng/ dee cooh-zee-neh		

Grammar note: English is a Germanic language, so this week's vocabulary provides some great examples of similar words in both languages. As you continue to study German, you will see more similarities between the two languages.

Cultural note: Germany is a country filled with storybook castles. Lichtenstein Castle, built atop a tall cliff, is one example of beautiful architecture from hundreds of years ago.

Idea! Go through your family album and identify members of your family in German.

Week 23: His Name Is_____.

Review: Weeks 20-22: Meet My Family (A,B,C)

Vocabulary:

>Ich heisse…   (My name is…)
>*eech hi-sseh*

>Er heisst…   (His name is…)
>*ehr hi-sst*

>Sie heisst…   (Her name is…)
>*see hi-st*

Grammar note: Sometimes the phrasing in another language is different than what we are used to in English. While "Mein Name ist Bond, James Bond" is the official translation, it is an "ancient" formal form that today nobody uses anymore.

Cultural note: The Biedermeir style of painting was very popular in the early nineteenth century. These paintings showed happy times, family life and charming images. A good example is *Cactus Friend,* by Carl Spitzweg.

Idea! Go around the dinner table and tell your own name and the name of the person on the right.

Week 24: Review

- Review vocabulary and concepts from weeks 17-23.

    o Now you have the phrases, "Wer ist das....?" and "Wo ist...?" under your belt. These are two of the quickest ways to do impromptu reviews anywhere! Use them whenever you think of them.

    o Throw an old magazine in your car. When you have some wait time at pick ups or drop offs, ask kids to point to der tisch, die tür,etc

    o Have a camera phone or digital camera? Let your kids scroll through the pictures as long as they are verbally labeling all the family members they see.

- Learn more about the arts in Germany!

    o Get a book on artists of the Northern Renaissance out from the library.

    o Look up images of the beautiful varied examples of German architecture.

    o Read a children's version of Beethoven's incredible life story.

    o Watch a performance of one of Wagner's operas on YouTube.

    o Read about the Bauhaus movement.

    o Take out CD's from the library and explore the enormous selection of German composed music.

Unit 4: Useful Information

Week 25: Days of the Week

Review: Review Weeks 17-24

Vocabulary:

Montag   (Monday)
mohn-tahg

Dienstag   (Tuesday)
deens-tahg

Mittwoch   (Wednesday)
Meet-vohch

Donnerstag   (Thursday)
Dohnnehrs-tahg

Freitag   (Friday)
Fri-tahg

Samstag   (Saturday)
Sahms-tahg

Sonntag   (Sunday)
Sohn-tahg

Grammar note: The days of the week in German are capitalized as they are in English, because they are nouns.

Example:

Heute ist Montag. (Today is Monday.)

Cultural note: Germany is famous for its sausages. They make over 1000 different kinds of sausage! The North American "frankfurter" or "hot dog" is derived from German sausages.

Idea! Write the days of the week on index cards and put them all in an envelope. Let your children take turns taking out the correct day of the week and hanging it on the fridge with a magnet.

Week 26: What Day is Today?

Review: Week 25: Days of the Week

Vocabulary:

> Welcher Tag ist heute?   (What day is today?)
> *Vehl-chehr tahg eest hoi-teh*

Grammar note: Because German nouns have one of three genders, the questioning word needs to fit with the respective noun.

The word for day is masculine: *der* Tag. When we question, we use the masculine form of "what": *Welcher* Tag.

The word for "week" is feminine: *die* Woche. If we were asking "What week?", we would use the feminine form: *Welche* Woche.

Cultural note: Do you like cookies? Germany has some of the most delicious traditional cookies you have ever tasted! From the spicy gingerbread *lebkuchen* to buttery *butterplatchen* to the cinnamon deliciousness of *zimsterne*, German bakers know how to make great cookies!

Idea! Ask your kids each morning before they start their day, *"Welcher Tag ist heute?"*

Week 27:Numbers 1-10

Review: Week 5: How Old Are You?

Vocabulary:
null (zero)
noohl

eins (one)
ins

zwei (two)
tsvi

drei (three)
dri

vier (four)
feer

fünf (five)
fuenf

sechs (six)
zehchs

sieben (seven)
zee-behn

acht (eight)
ahcht

neun (nine)
noin

zehn (ten)
tsehn

Pronunciation note: Remember that the *h* after a vowel indicates that it is spoken longer. The letter "z" in German is spoken very hard, like the hiss of a snake.

Cultural note: Have you ever had a hot dog with *sauerkraut*? Sauerkraut means "sour cabbage" in Germany and originated there.

Idea! Use playing card to help kids memorize their numbers. Hold up a card and if the child says the correct number in German, they get to keep the card. Make the joker worth *null* and the jack, queen and king worth *zehn*.

Week 28: How Many?

Review: Week 27: Numbers 0-10

Vocabulary:

>Wie viel(e)?   (How many?)
>*Vee fee-leh*

Grammar note: In order to be able to speak any language, you need to know key question words. Now you can add *wie viel(e)* to your existing repertoire of *wer, was, wo, wann, welche(r,s)* and *wie*. You can get quite a lot of information with these simple words!

Cultural note: Germans love their bread and they traditionally make a darker bread. One popular German bread is pumpernickel, which is like a dark rye bread.

Idea! Review previous vocabulary through counting. *Wie viele Fenster? Wie viel Jungen?*

Week 29: Months

Review: Week 25: Days of the Week

Vocabulary:

Januar (January)
Yah-nooh-ahr

Februar (February)
Feh-brooh-ahr

März (March)
Marts

April (April)
Ah-preel

Mai (May)
Mi

Juni (June)
Yooh-nee

Juli (July)
Yooh-lee

August (August)
Ow-guhst

September (September)
Zehp-tehm-behr

Oktober (October)
Ohk-toh-behr

November (November)
Noh-vehm-behr

Dezember   (December)
Deh-tsehm-behr

Grammar note: As you have probably noted from previous lessons, many words are the same in both German and English, just with different pronunciation. Other words are extremely similar. As a matter of fact, the English and German languages have common origins. So you already know more German than you think!

Cultural Note: Germany is famous all over the world for its fine beers and wines.

Idea! Many German names for the months sound similar to their English counterparts. Use this similarity to help your kids memorize them. Give your children a clue and they have to guess the month you are talking about in English:

Clue: We trick or treat in Oktober. Answer: October

Clue: We fly kites in *März*. Answer: March

Week 30: I Know.....

Review: Weeks 25 & 29: Days and Months of the Year

Vocabulary:

> Ich kenne…   (I know…)
> *Eech keh-neh*

> die Tage der Woche!   (the days of the week!)
> *dee tah-geh dehr voh-cheh*

> die Monate des Jahres!   (the months of the year!)
> *dee moh-nah-the dehs yah-rehs*

Pronunciation note: Remember that in German no letter is silent – not even the "e" at the end of words! Remember to stress the second to last syllable.

Cultural note: Hamburgers are enjoyed all over the world, but they originated in Hamburg, Germany, which is how they got their name!

Idea! Let your kids brag! Encourage them to tell Grandma, or their teacher, or friend that they know the days of the week and the months of the year in German. Every time they use their German to communicate (even to brag a little) they are learning more of the language!

Week 31: When Is Your Birthday?

Review: Week 29: Months of the Year

Vocabulary:

Wann ist Dein Geburtstag?　　(When is your birthday?)

Vahn eest din geh-boohrts-tahg

Mein Geburtstag ist im (Mai).　(My birthday is in…..)
Min geh-boohrts-tahg eest eem　(mi)

Grammar note: Here we are using the familiar form of *your*, *Dein*. You would probably know someone fairly well if you were asking them their birthday! If you were asking a teacher, for example, you would use the formal your, *Ihr.*

Cultural note: One sweet treat that came from Germany is a favorite with children all over the world…Gummi Bears! The first Gummi Bears were produced by the German candy company, Haribo in 1920.

Idea! If your child's birthday is between 1-10 let them try to figure out how they would say the date of their birth: *"Mein Geburtstag ist am 4. Juli"*. If their birthday is a bigger number, help them look up the number and figure it out!

Week 32: Review

- Learning all this useful information requires a lot of memorization.

  - Use playing cards or preschool counting flashcards to review numbers.
  - Count cars on the road. How many…trucks, red cars, motorcycles, etc.
  - Practice your days of the week song or create your own.
  - Try some fun games and videos available online. Check out the games on digitaldialects.com/german and bbc.co.uk/schools/primarylanguages/german
  - Have a group birthday party. Bake (or buy) a delicious Black Forest cake. Everyone has to state their birthday in order to get a taste.

- Learn more about the food of Germany

  - Grill up some bratwurst for dinner.
  - Visit a German restaurant.
  - See if your local supermarket carries traditional German potato dumplings.
  - Taste an apple strudel!
  - Enjoy a sandwich on pumpernickel for lunch.
  - Next time you want to make cookies try making *spritz* instead of chocolate chip.

Unit 5: Mealtimes

Week 33: I'm Hungry

Review: Concepts from Weeks 25-32

Vocabulary:

Hast Du Hunger?	(Are you hungry?)
Hahst dooh hoohn-gehr	
Ich habe Hunger	(I'm hungry.)
Eech hah-beh hoohn-gehr	

Grammar note: In German, to express a negative answer, you add a form of the word *kein*, which can mean no, none or not at all. In this example we use the form, *keinen.*

Example:

Hast Du Hunger?   *Nein. Ich habe keinen Hunger.*

Are you hungry?   No. I'm not hungry at all.

Cultural note: Albrecht Dürer was a famous German artist who lived in the sixteenth century. He is considered by many to be the greatest artist of his time. Dürer was a painter, engraver, printmaker, mathematician and an author.

Idea! This is one of the easiest conversations to practice because we all have meals every day! Incorporate this simple question into your regular mealtimes.

Week 34: Favorite Foods

Review: Week 33: I'm Hungry

Vocabulary:

das Brot	(bread)
dahs broht	
der Apfel	(apple)
dehr ahp-fehl	
die Marmelade	(jam)
dee mahrmeh-lahdeh	
der Käse	(cheese)
dehr ka-zeh	
die Kekse	(cookies)
dee kehk-zeh	
die Karotten	(carrots)
dee kah-roh-teh	

Pronunciation note: The *ä* is another *umlaute*, a very German sound. It is pronounced like a combination of the *a* in say and the *e* in melon.

Cultural note: Most people have heard of Ludwig von Beethoven, the famous deaf composer. In spite of his hearing loss, Beethoven went on to compose some of the most beautiful music the world has ever heard.

Idea! Brainstorm your own list of favorite foods. Your kids will learn their own favorites quicker if they have to ask for them in German in order to receive them!

Week 35: I Like......

Review: Week 34: Favorite Foods

Vocabulary:

Magst Du..	(Do you like…?)
Mahgst dooh	
Ich mag	(I like….)
Eech mahg	

Grammar note: The words *magst* and *mag* are two forms of the verb *mögen*, which means, to like. In German, the verb changes depending on who is the subject of the sentence.

Cultural note: Rainer Maria Rilke was a famous German lyrical poet. Some of his most famous poems are the "Duino Elegies", a group of ten poems that speak of the importance of beauty.

Idea! You can have a lot of fun practicing this concept. Tell the children they are having horrible things for breakfast, lunch, or dinner and innocently ask them, *"Magst Du…?"* They can respond with an emphatic, *"Nein!"*

Week 36: I'm Thirsty!

Review: Week 33: I'm Hungry!

Vocabulary:

> Hast Du Durst ?   (Are you   thirsty?)
> *Hahst dooh doohrst*
>
> Ich habe Durst.   (I'm thirsty.)
> *Eech hah-beh doohrst*

Grammar note: Translations between languages are not word for word. Literally, *Hast Du Durst?* means, "Have you thirst?". When we translate for meaning, we say the phrase the natural way an English speaker would, "Are you thirsty?".

Cultural note: One of the most famous physicists in the world is Albert Einstein. Among his work, Einstein discovered the "Theory of Relativity" which changed the field of physics.

Idea! A hot summer's day is a great time to make a pitcher of lemonade and see who is thirsty. Weather not warm? Try and make some hot cocoa instead!

Week 37: Can I Have......?

Review: Week 34: Favorite Foods

Vocabulary:

Ich hätte gern, _____, bitte.   (I would like_____please?)
Eech ha-teh gehrn_____, bee-teh

Grammar note: As in English, there is more than one way to request things in German. Just like in English, it is important to ask politely, adding *bitte*, or please.

Cultural note: Boris Becker is a famous tennis player. He was the youngest player ever to win the Wimbleton title, at only seventeen.

Idea! Make snack time practice time! Let your children pick their own afternoon snack and then ask for it – in *deutsch*-of course!

Week 38: Sit at the Table

Review: Week 37: Can I Have…?

Vocabulary:

> Setz(t) Dich/euch! (Sit at the table.)
> *Zehts deech/ zehtst oich*

Pronunciation note: The sound of *s* is pronounced like a *z* in German.

Cultural note: Johannes Gutenberg was a fourteenth century inventor who created a way to print the written word. This invention changed the world.

Idea! Assign a "dinner helper" who gets the rest of the family to the table each night. Pick a different dinner helper every night so each child gets a chance to practice using and listening to this command.

Week 39: Where Is My.....?

Review: Week 38: Sit Down at the Table.

Vocabulary:

die Tasse *Dee tah-sseh*	(cup)
die Gabel *dee gah-behl*	(fork)
das Messer *dahs meh-ssehr*	(knife)
der Löffel *dehr lu-fehl*	(spoon)
und *oohnd*	(and)

Pronunciation note: Remember, those *umlaute* sounds are different from anything in English. Try for a sound like an *ee* but with your lips rounded. Listening online to native speakers speak the alphabet sounds is very helpful when trying to pronounce these German sounds.

Cultural note: Otto Hahn was a world famous chemist. He won the Nobel Prize for his work in the field of nuclear chemistry.

Idea! Pair up different items you have previously learned using your new word *und*. Play *Mama hat gesagt* with two items instead of one.

Example: *Mama hat gesagt, "Fass an Deine Nase und an Deinen Mund".*

Week 40: Review

- Mealtime vocabulary is some of the easiest vocabulary to learn. Practice times occur every day so it feels easy and natural to incorporate these words. In addition, children enjoy learning and using the names of their favorite foods.

  o At a restaurant, see if you can translate any items on the menu.
  o Mix your old vocabulary with new. When asked, *"Wie geht es Ihnen/Dir?"* you can respond, *"Ich habe Hunger.* You can use the phrase, *"Wo ist ...?"* to locate food items on the table.

- Learn more about some famous German people.

  o Visit your local library and take out biographies on famous German citizens. There are too many to name!
  o Go to biography.com to find a wide selection of stories about men, women and children from Germany.

- The contributions the German have made in science, literature, world affairs and music and art is incredible. German people have had an enormous impact on the world. Check out how Germans have influenced your favorite subject.

Unit 6: Getting Ready

Week 41: Wake Up!

Review: Vocabulary and concepts from weeks 32-39.

Vocabulary:

> Wach(t) auf!　　　　　(Wake up!)
> *Vahch(t) owf*

> Guten morgen, mein Kind!　(Good morning ,my child!)
> *Gooh-tehn mohr-gehn, min keend*

Grammar note: If you want to greet more than one of your children, you will have to change this phrase to the plural:

Guten morgen, Kinder! (Good morning children!)

Cultural note: German is not only spoken in Germany! Germany is the dominant language of Austria, Switzerland and Liechtenstien as well as Germany. There are countries all over the world where Germany is used. Throughout the world, 96 million people speak German!

Idea! Start your day in German! Wake your children every day with a cheery, *"Guten Morgen Kinder!"*.

Week 42: Getting Ready

Review: Week 41: Wake Up!

Vocabulary:

> Ich wasche mein Gesicht.　　(I wash my face.)
> *Eech va-sheh min geh-seecht*

> Ich putze meine Zähne.　　(I brush my teeth.)
> *Eech pooh-tseh mi-neh tsa-neh*

> Ich ziehe mich an.　　(I get dressed.)
> *Eech tsee-eh meech ahn*

Grammar: When we are writing or speaking about parts of the body we use the articles *der, die, or das* instead of the pronoun *mein or meine.* In English, this is the equivalent of saying, "I wash the face" instead of "I wash my face". It is just a different way of phrasing, but means the same thing.

Cultural note: Germany is a land of innovators. The history of the fields of science, mathematics, engineering, linguistics, literature or art is filled with German people. Their contributions to the world are too many to list here!

Idea! Have your child tell you what he has to do in the morning before he leaves for school or otherwise starts his day.

Week 43: I Want To Wear.....(A)

Review: Week 42: Getting Ready

Vocabulary:

Ich möchte......anziehen.   (I want to wear....)
Eech much-teh   ahn-tsee-ehn

ein T-shirt   (tee shirt)
in t-shirt

eine Hose   (pants)
i-neh hoh-zeh

ein Kleid   (dress)
in klid

ein Rock   (skirt)
in rohk

eine kurze Hose   (shorts)
i-neh koohr-tseh hoh-zeh

Grammar note: Remember number agreement. You must match your pronoun or article to your noun.

Cultural note: German is the most widely spoken language in Europe.

Idea! Before you put your kids to bed, help them pick out their outfits using their German vocabulary.

Week 44: I Want To Wear ...(B)

Review: Week 43: I Want To Wear....(A)

Vocabulary:

rosa/pink *roh-sah/ peenk*	(pink)
rot *roht*	(red)
blau *blow*	(blue)
grün *gruen*	(green)
weiss *viss*	(white)
schwarz *shvahrts*	(black)
organge *orahngj*	(orange)
gelb *gehlb*	(yellow)
lila/violet *lee-lah/veeo-leht*	(purple)

Grammar note: Using the colors in German can be a little confusing!

Generally, when the color precedes the noun, it changes according to the gender of the noun.

When the color word comes after the noun, it does not change.

The color does not change form when it ends in –la.

Lastly, the color always ends in e when it is preceded by the articles der/die/das.

As you learn to speak a language, these special rules become natural and you remember them automatically. Don't worry if you get confused at this early stage!

Cultural note: Over half a million people speak German in Brazil.

Idea! Play *I Spy* using your new color words. Of course, when we are studying German we don't play *I Spy* we play *Ich sehe was, was Du nicht siehst und das ist....* (I see something you don't see! And that something is…).

Week 45: Where Are Your Shoes?

Review: Week 44: I Want To Wear…(B).

Vocabulary:

> Wo sind Deine Schuhe?   (Where are your shoes?)
> *Voh zeend di-neh shooh-eh*
>
> Hier sind sie (doch)!   (Here they are!)
> *Heer zeend see (dohch)*

Pronunciation note: In German, *sch* is pronounced the same as the English *sh*.

Cultural note: Oktoberfest is a festival celebrated in many parts of the United States. It originated in Germany.

Idea! Hide some everyday items and make the phrase, *Wo sind..?* the start of a treasure hunt!

Week 46: Let's Hurry Up!

Review: Weeks 2 and 6: Greetings

Vocabulary:

> Beeil Dich!   (Let's hurry up!)
> *Beh-il deech*

Grammar note: Beeil Dich is used when you are talking to one person. If you need to hustle your whole family out the door, say, *Beeilt euch (beh-ilt oich)*!

Cultural note: Many of the world's most popular automobiles were designed in Germany. Mercedes-Benz and Volkswagon are both German designed cars.

Idea! Give each child a turn to sound the morning alarm. Let them announce, *Beeilt euch!* Maybe it will help get you out of the house on time!

Week 47: Have a Good Day!

Review: Week 46: It's Time to Go!

Vocabulary:

Einen schönen Tag.   (Have a nice day!)
i-nehn shu-nehn tahg

Pronunciaton note: In German, when wishing someone a good night (Gute Nacht) or day the sentence looks like a statement only.

Cultural note: There are communities in North America where German is still the dominant language. The communities of Amish, Mennonite or Hutterite people use German regularly.

Idea! Find a German restaurant and get lunch. Make sure to wish the waiter, Einen schönen Tag".

Week 48: Review

- Review all the vocabulary and concepts from the past weeks.

  - Incorporate your new vocabulary when getting
  - dressed every day.
  - Pretend! Play puppets, paper dolls or Barbies with your kids and use your German vocabulary to get them dressed.
  - Label clothing you see in stores when you are out
  - shopping.

- Learn more about German culture around the world!

  - Make a book out of the flags of countries where German is spoken.
  - Listen to some German music. There are many varieties!
  - "Pin" a map! Get a world map, and help your child put a pushpin into all the countries where German is spoken around the world.
  - Watch an Oompah band on Youtube.com
  - Google images of the Germany's Black Forest.
  - Visit a clock store and admire the different cuckoo clocks.

Unit 7: A Few Odds and Ends

Week 49: Things Around the House

Review: Vocabulary from Weeks 41-47

Vocabulary:

> das Bett   (bed)
> *dahs beht*
>
> das Sofa   (sofa)
> *dahs zoh-fah*
>
> die Lampe   (lamp)
> *dee lahm-peh*
>
> das Telefon   (telephone)
> *dahs tehleh-fohn*
>
> der Computer   (computer)
> *dehr cohmpyooh-tehr*

Grammar note: What to sound really German? Refer to your computer as a *Rechner (resh-nehr)*. This is a more colloquial way of saying computer.

Cultural note: Do you like fairy tales? Many well known of your favorite fairy tales originated in the *Grimm's Fairy Tales*. *Rapunzel, Snow White* and *Hansel and Gretel* all began their rise to stardom in this famous book of children's stories.

Idea! Play *Heiss oder Kalt?* (Hot or Cold?). Play the same way you would play Hot or Cold? But instead of hiding an item, you simply think of one in the room and direct your children toward it by saying *heiss* or *kalt*. When they find it they have to tell you what it is in German. Then they get a turn!

Week 50: Things in Our World.

Review: Week 21: Who Is This?

Vocabulary:

Was ist das?   (What is this?)
Vahs eest dahs

der Bus   (bus)
Dehr boohs

das Auto   (car)
dahs ow-toh

der Himmel   (sky)
dehr hee-mehl

die Strasse   (street)
dee strah-seh

die Leute   (people)
dee loi-teh

der Zug   (train)
dehr tsoohg

der Fluss   (river)
dehr floohss

die Blume   (flower)
dee blooh-meh

der Baum   (tree)
dehr bowm

Grammar note: Remember, if you want to say *the*, you use *der, die* or *das*.

If you want to say *a*, you use *ein* or *eine*.

Example: Das ist eine Blume. = It is a flower.

Das ist die Blume. = It is the flower.

Cultural note: The first printed book came from Germany!

Idea! Use the question, *Was ist das?* to practice mixing up your articles and pronouns. Try different ways of answering the same question:

It is my car/ It is the car. *Das ist mein Auto./Das ist das Auto.*

It is a train/It is the train. *Das ist ein Zug./Das ist der Zug.*

Week 51: Places We Go

Review: Week 50: Things in Our World

Vocabulary:

Gehen wir zu(m,r)…….	(Let's go to…..)
Geh-ehn veer tsooh(m,r)	
die Schule	(school)
dee shooh-leh	
das Lokal/Restaurant	(restaurant)
dahs loh-kahl/ rehs-tow-rahnt	
das Geschäft/der Laden	(store)
dahs geh-shaft/ dehr lah-dehn	
der Strand	(beach)
dehr strahnd	
der Park	(park)
dehr pahrk	
das Kino	(movies)
dahs kee-noh	
die Bank	(bank)
dee bahnk	

Grammar note: The word *zum* is used in this phrase for masculine and neutral nouns: *Gehen wir zum Strand*. (Let's go to the beach.)

The word *zur* is used for feminine nouns: *Gehen wir zur Schule.* (Let's go to the school.)

Cultural note: There are over 300 kinds of bread in Germany. Germans love their bread so much there is even a bread museum in Ulm, Germany.

Idea! Make running errands a learning experience. Narrate where you are headed as you run around town and let your kids translate before you get there!

Week 52: Review

- Review your vocabulary from weeks 49-51.
- Have a *feier!* You did it! A year of studying a foreign language is no small feat. Plan a party for you and your children. Incorporate some of the foods and customs you have learned about over the past year. Don't be afraid to mix and match!
- Keep practicing your German vocabulary. The more you speak, the more you will retain.
- Keep learning! Read German language storybooks. Listen to German songs and music. Hopefully you have embarked on a love affair with this new language. Keep your curiosity piqued and bring your children along for the ride!

Where Do I Go From Here?

Here you are, a year or so later with a good deal of spoken vocabulary in your pocket. What's next? That question can only be answered by you. The key to mastering any language is to continue speaking it. No amount of studying can make you fluent if you don't reach out to others and try to communicate. Continue to make learning German a family affair. You will always have study buddies and you will be giving your children a priceless gift. Utilize the internet to find others who are interested in practicing their German. Join social groups and take daily opportunities to use the German you have already obtained.

For more formal instruction, you can register for inexpensive courses online through any number of companies. There are many companies operating out of German speaking countries that offer lessons through Skype for just a few dollars a lesson. Many libraries have audio and computer courses available to lend.

Another affordable option is to attend local community German courses for adult learners. Most communities offer seasonal enrichment courses, and Beginner's German may be offered in your area. You may meet other people interested in learning German with whom you can practice.

If you are very goal oriented, or want to receive certification of some sort, you can attend classes at a community college where you live. This will certainly increase your knowledge of written German. Course offerings vary and usually don't extend beyond beginner-intermediate levels.

There are so many free resources available nowadays online that you can easily continue your German language learning on your own time. The next section outlines many free resources you can use to increase your German skills.

Learning Resources

All websites, smart phone applications and podcasts listed below are available for free. Books and music should be available at most local libraries.

Internet Sites

familylanguageresources.com: A collection of links to free learning websites, free lesson plans, free worksheets and curriculum to pace your instruction. The site also has a section of reviewed learning materials; books, cds and curriculum packages.

YouTube.com: We all love youtube.com for funny emails but it really is an invaluable teaching resource when you want to learn about or expose your children to different cultures.

googletranslate.com: Hit this site for quick general translations.

livemocha.com: Do you like Facebook? This site is designed to promote communication with language learners all over the world. You can email or chat with members in English or German. Complimentary lessons are available. You can also earn "money" towards fee based lessons by correcting the lessons of English language learners. In addition, great pictures taken by locals of foreign countries all over the world are available for viewing in the "Explore Culture" section.

bbc.co.uk/schools/primarylanguages/German: This is a terrific site for children. German vocabulary is divided up into topics.

Explanations are provided for each topic, and corresponding games are available to reinforce learning.

digitaldialects.com: This site presents a selection of fun, engaging German vocabulary building games.

webgerman.com: A collection of links, printables games and literature you can use to supplement your German program.

Apps

MindSnacks Learn German has some really fun games if you want to develop your visual knowledge of the German language. Oral presentation of words is also included with a native accent.

iTranslate is a great feature to keep on your phone. If you want to add to your personal repertoire, or are trying to have small conversations with native speakers, you just type in the word you want to say and it gives you a translation. You can also hit an icon next to the phrase to hear it spoken with proper pronunciation.

Duolingo is an app containing wonderful vocabulary and grammar building games. You can slow down the speed to make the words easier to understand.

Podcasts

Listening to podcasts in German is a great way to improve your understanding of spoken language.

Of interest to adults:

Coffeebreakgerman.com: A terrific resource for boosting your listening comprehension, and achieving verbal skills. This is a course consisting of short lessons that are aimed at beginners. You can access this free course through iTunes or go to their website at mydailyphrase.com.

oneminutegerman.com: Also brought to you by Radiolingua, this course is for absolute beginners. In it, you will learn basic words and phrases that will help you if you are planning a trip to Germany, or just want to get started learning German.

Slowgerman.com: A native speaker presents podcasts spoken in slow, clearly enunciated German. There is a section for "Absolute Beginners" which is a great place to start listening.

For children:

Podbean.com: This site provides stories in German for children, spoken by children. There are a great variety of podcasts to choose from.

wdrmaus.de: Based on the famous German television mouse, this site hosts games and podcasts in German for children.

Books

Usborne Books is a publishing company that has created many bright, colorful and interactive German language books for children. Some of their titles are aimed at the youngest children, and contain interactive features like lift-a-flap. Other books are designed to engage older children. Check out their complete selection of titles at myubam.com. Many local libraries carry their books.

Look What Came from Germany, Kevin Davis: This bright and colorful book introduces children to Germany in an interesting way.

German for Beginners, Angela Wilkes: This introductory guide to German is illustrated by John Shackell and teaches everyday German.

Music

Putting on CD's in the car can really pump up listening comprehension.

Kindergarden Music: The 30 Best German Songs for Children, by Kindergarden Music, has a nice selection of children's music. You can purchase the CD online or as individual song downloads.

20 Best Loved German Folk Songs, by Robert Cornman, is another wonderful CD to add to your German music collection. This CD is also available in its entirety or you can purchase individual songs

ABOUT THE AUTHOR

Eileen Mc Aree is a teacher, writer and mother. She lives in New York with her husband, four kids and their dog, Biscuit.

24741541R00049

Made in the USA
San Bernardino, CA
04 October 2015